THE WORLD'S SMARTEST ANIMALS

CROWS

by Ruth Owen

WINDMILL BOOKS

New York

Published in 2012 by Windmill Books, An Imprint of Rosen Publishing
29 East 21st Street, New York, NY 10010

Editor for Ruby Tuesday Books Ltd: Mark J. Sachner
U.S. Editor: Sara Antill
Designer: Emma Randall
Consultant: Kevin J. McGowan, Cornell Laboratory of Ornithology

Cover, 1, 4, 6, 7 (top left), 7 (center), 7 (bottom left), 7 (bottom right), 8, 12, 20–21, 22–23, 24–25, 27, 28–29, 30 © Shutterstock; 5, 10–11 © FLPA; 7 (top right), 9 © Wikipedia Creative Commons (public domain); 13 © Bruce Coleman Photography; 14–15 © Superstock; 16–17 © Geoff Robinson Photography/Chris Bird; 19 © Christopher Bird/PA Photos.

Library of Congress Cataloging-in-Publication Data

Owen, Ruth, 1967–
 Crows / by Ruth Owen.
    p. cm. — (The world's smartest animals)
 Includes index.
 ISBN 978-1-61533-376-9 (library binding) — ISBN 978-1-61533-414-8 (pbk.) —
ISBN 978-1-61533-473-5 (6-pack)
 1. Crows—Juvenile literature. I. Title.
 QL696.P2367O94 2012
 598.8'64—dc22

                                    2011014574

Manufactured in the United States of America

CPSIA Compliance Information: Batch #RTS1102WM: For Further Information contact Windmill Books, New York, New York at 1-866-478-0556

CONTENTS

MEET THE FAMILY

It's early evening.
A mother is busy giving her three youngsters something to eat.
Dad and the family's older daughter are helping, too.
A grown-up son arrives home.
He's been out of town for the day.
Everyone is chatting loudly.
You might think that this is a human family, but in fact,
it's a family of **American crows**!

Not everyone likes crows. Some people say they are **pests** because they eat crops. Others don't like them because they live in large, noisy groups. However, crows are some of the smartest animals on Earth!

Crows can solve problems. They can even use **tools**. Crows have also learned to live alongside people and use us as a way of finding lots of different foods!

An American crow

4

Crows will work as a team to get food. If they spot a bird feeder filled with seeds, one crow might land on the feeder and rock it from side to side. Other crows will wait beneath the feeder to catch the seeds!

CROW SKILLS

A family of American crows

ALL ABOUT CROWS

Crows belong to a bird family that scientists call the corvids. It is also simply known as the crow family.

The crow family includes the many different types of actual crows, such as the American crow, the fish crow, and the hooded crow. It also includes rooks and different types of ravens, jays, magpies, and jackdaws. Members of the crow family live in almost every part of the world. They live in the countryside, at the seashore, and in cities.

Members of the crow family eat lots of different foods. They eat nuts, seeds, grain, and fruit. They also eat eggs, worms, insects, small animals such as frogs and mice, and **carrion**, the bodies of dead animals. Crows will also break into trash cans and garbage bags to eat people's leftover food.

Common raven

CROW SKILLS

Ravens are the biggest members of the crow family. A raven's wingspan, the measurement from wing tip to wing tip, can reach nearly 5 feet (1.5 m).

European magpie

Hooded crow

Florida scrub jay

Rook

European jackdaw

7

SMART WITH FOOD

All the members of the crow family store spare food. They might hide it in a tree, or they might cover the food with grass or leaves and hide it on the ground.

Western scrub jays will keep watch to see if other jays are watching them hide food. If they suspect they are being watched, they will pretend to hide food by putting their beaks to the ground. The other birds won't know which is the real stash of food and which is fake!

Some crows catch and eat fish. In Finland and Sweden, people cut fishing holes through the ice on lakes and ponds. Then they leave fishing lines dangling in the water below. Crows pull the fishing lines out of the holes and eat the fish!

A flock of rooks follows a tractor in order to pick up worms and grubs from the plowed soil.

CROW SKILLS

Crows will eat shellfish. On the Scottish island of Rum, hooded crows pick up shellfish, such as mussels, from the beaches and shallow waters. The crows then fly up into the air and drop the shellfish onto rocks to crack open the shells.

A hooded crow looks for food in a bag of garbage.

SAFETY iN NUMBERS

During the fall and winter, American crows often spend the night in huge groups called roosts.

A roost might include a few hundred crows or thousands of them. One roost in Oklahoma was believed to include around two million crows!

Scientists don't know for sure why crows sleep in large roosts. It could be that there's safety in numbers. **Predators**, such as great horned owls, will attack crows. A crow is safer if it is one of thousands of other crows than if it's in a tree on its own.

Crows might even stick together so that they can spy on each other. If their neighbors find a good feeding place, such as a farm or garbage dump, the other crows can follow them in the morning!

Before nightfall, crows gather in places away from the roost. They spend time shouting to each other, fighting, and chasing each other in the sky. Then, as darkness falls, the huge flocks of crows fly together to their roosting place.

CROW SKILLS

As night falls, crows gather, ready to return to their roost.

CROW FAMILIES

Most members of the crow family find a partner, or mate, and stay with that mate for life. When it is time to have young, the crow couple builds a nest.

A female American crow will normally lay four or five eggs at a time. After the crow chicks hatch from their eggs, their parents bring them food. The chicks spend up to six weeks in the nest. Then they learn to fly. Young birds that are old enough to leave the nest are called fledglings. After leaving the nest, the fledglings learn how to find their own food.

Some American crows stay with their parents for five or even six years. During this time, they act as helpers. They help defend their parents' nests from predators. They bring food to their mother when she is sitting on eggs. They will also help feed younger brothers and sisters once they hatch.

This jackdaw is collecting sticks to build a nest.

Building a nest can take up to two weeks. The parents and their helpers work together. The nest is made from sticks with an inside layer of grass and mud. The mother makes a soft bed for her eggs using tree bark, plants, or animal fur. Sometimes, she might use plastic, paper, or twine.

A nest of American crow chicks

CLEVER CROWS USE TOOLS

One way that members of the crow family show how smart they are is by using tools.

This shows us that the crows are smart enough to understand when they cannot carry out a task. They solve problems by finding, or even making, tools that allow them to carry out tasks.

New Caledonian crows use twigs to dig grubs out of holes in trees. Scientists wanted to know more about this. The crows are shy, however, and live in thick forests. Scientists invented a tiny camera that weighs as much as a paper clip. They then caught 18 crows and attached cameras to their tails. The tiny cameras showed crows carefully choosing twigs. Then the crows pulled the leaves off the twigs to make them smooth. Finally, they used their beaks to make the ends of the sticks into hooks.

New Caledonian crows use stems of dry grass to dig for food on the ground. Scientists think they might be digging for ants. The crows also tear up leaves to make pointed tools. Sometimes they keep a good tool to use again in the future!

CROW SKILLS

A New Caledonian crow uses a stick to dig for grubs in a tree trunk.

EXTRA-SMART TOOL MAKERS

In the UK, an experiment was carried out with a group of four rooks. The rooks had been raised by people. They had not learned any skills from other rooks.

Each rook was given a small bucket of worms at the bottom of a tube. The rooks couldn't reach the buckets with their beaks, though. The rooks were also given pieces of wire. Each bird bent the wire to make a hook. They then pulled the buckets up with the hooks. The rooks made tools to solve the problem!

The four rooks had never seen another bird do this. Each rook figured it out for itself. They also didn't need lots of tries to get it right. Three of the rooks made a wire hook on their first try!

The rook sees the straight piece of wire.

A tube containing a bucket of worms

Piece of wire

16

CROW SKILLS

Betty, a New Caledonian crow, was being studied at a university in the UK. Betty could use hooks to get food from difficult places. One day, Betty was given some meat in a tube. The meat was out of reach. Instead of a hook, Betty was given a straight piece of wire. Smart Betty bent the wire to make herself a hook!

The rook makes a hook from the wire so it can reach the bucket of worms!

BRAINY BIRDS SOLVE PROBLEMS

The four tool-making rooks also showed scientists that they could solve tricky problems.

Each rook was given a tube that contained some water. A tasty worm was floating in the water. The water in the tube was too low for the rook to reach the worm with its beak, though.

The scientists then gave each rook a little pile of stones. One by one, each rook dropped some stones into the tube, which raised the water level. The rooks kept adding stones until the water was high enough to reach the worm!

Two rooks named Connelly and Monroe needed two tries to get this test right. The other two rooks, Cook and Fry, solved the problem on their first try!

CROW SKILLS

Pairs of rooks were given a tray of food outside their cage. A piece of string was threaded through hooks on the tray. The two ends of the string were put into the cage. The rooks figured out that they each needed to pull on one end of the string to pull the tray over to the cage!

These photographs have been taken from a video. The video shows a rook using stones to raise the water level in a tube.

THAT'S NUTS!

In Japan, a group of crows invented a smart way to crack the hard shells on nuts.

First, a crow drops a nut onto a road. Then, it waits for a car to run over the nut and crack the shell! Eating nuts on a busy road can be dangerous, however. The crows have learned to drop the nuts onto pedestrian crosswalks. The cars crush the nuts. Then, when the green walk light flashes, the crows walk onto the crosswalk and eat their nuts in safety!

The crows not only solved the problem of how to crack nuts. They were also smart enough to learn how pedestrian crosswalks work and use them to get food!

Large numbers of crows in the area now use cars as a way to crack nuts. The crows are learning from other crows how to do this. Youngsters are also learning from their parents.

CROW SKILLS

SO HOW SMART ARE CROWS?

Crows are smart enough to quickly solve problems they have never faced before. They are also able to think through a complicated plan of action.

A New Caledonian crow was presented with some food in a long tube. The crow was also given a short hook. However, the hook wasn't long enough to reach the food. What the crow needed was a long hook.

Inside some other tubes were a medium-length hook and a long hook. However, the long hook was also out of reach. The crow used the short hook to pull the medium hook from its tube. Then it used the medium hook to reach the long hook. Finally, it was able to use the long hook to reach the food!

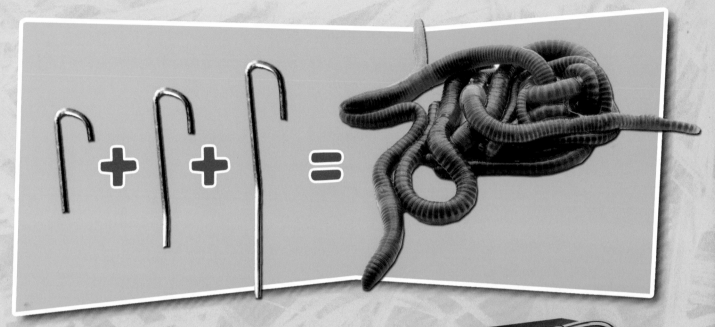

Many smart animals, such as crows, dolphins, and chimpanzees, live in large groups. You need to be smart to live in a group. You must make relationships. You also have to figure out who is a trusted friend, or who may want to steal your food or mate!

CROW SKILLS

Young crows play with sticks to learn how to use them for building nests.

CROWS AND PEOPLE

Crows can recognize individual humans. They remember people they like and people they think might be enemies.

Kevin McGowan is a scientist who studies crows. Sometimes he throws peanuts to the crows he is studying. The crows recognize McGowan as a friend and will chase after him, asking for peanuts.

Not all crows see McGowan as a friend, though. As part of his work, McGowan climbs up trees to the crows' nests. He puts small leg bands and markers on crow chicks so he can identify them in the future. This allows him to study what a crow does over many years. The crows don't like McGowan **tagging** their chicks. When these crows see McGowan around, they follow him and shout at him angrily!

CROW SKiLLS

If a predator comes too close to a crow's home, the crow will mob the predator. This means it will shout and fly at the predator again and again. The crow's shouts will attract other crows who will join the fight against the predator.

FRIEND OR FOE?

Scientists wanted to know if crows recognize people by their faces, their body shape, or even their smell.

At the University of Washington, scientists carried out an experiment. Different people captured and tagged seven crows while wearing the same caveman Halloween mask. Then, people who had not tagged any crows put on the mask and walked around outside the university. It didn't matter if the person in the mask was a man or a woman, tall or short, skinny or fat. The crows shouted at that person.

This showed the scientists that the crows remembered the caveman face. They weren't identifying their enemy by body shape or smell.

Over time, crows that had not been tagged also shouted at anyone wearing the caveman mask. These crows had learned from their parents and other crows that the caveman was an enemy!

Crows may have learned to recognize human faces as a way to survive. One person might feed them peanuts. Another might chase them or shoot at them. Knowing whom they can use to get food from or who might hurt them allows crows to live alongside people successfully.

CROW SKILLS

A friend with peanuts, an ugly Halloween mask face, or an angry farmer? Crows need to know who is a friend and who might be an enemy!

THE TOWER RAVENS

At the Tower of London, in England, there is a group of ravens with a special place in history.

According to **legend**, if the ravens leave the tower, the tower will fall and the kingdom will fall, too! King Charles II, who lived from 1630 to 1685, declared that there should always be six ravens living at the tower. The birds are cared for by the Ravenmaster.

The oldest raven to live at the tower was named Jim Crow. Jim was 44 when he died.

In 1986, George the raven was fired from his job at the tower. He'd been flying onto nearby roofs and damaging TV antennae. George was sent to live at a zoo in Wales.

The Tower of London, England

A Tower of London raven

CROW SKILLS

Thor the raven is very good at talking in a human voice. He copies the voice of the Ravenmaster. When visitors at the Tower of London hear Thor talking, they often think they have heard a person say something!

GLOSSARY

carrion (KAR-ee-un)
The dead and rotting body of an animal.

corvid (KOR-vid)
A member of the bird family known as corvids. The family includes crows, ravens, rooks, jackdaws, jays, and magpies. Corvids are the smartest of all the birds.

legend (LEH-jend)
A story that has been told and passed down through history. No one knows if the story is true or made up.

mate (MAYT)
An animal's partner that it produces young with. Some animals live with their mate for their whole lives, while others may only spend a few hours or days with a mate.

pest (PEST)
Something that is a nuisance or a problem because it causes damage. For example, an animal that eats a farmer's crops is a pest.

predator (PREH-duh-ter)
An animal that hunts and kills other animals for food.

tagging (TA-ging)
Attaching a small marker or tag to an animal's body so the animal can be identified and its daily life or movements recorded. Tagging can also mean putting a collar onto an animal, or a small band onto an animal's leg, for the same purpose.

tool (TOOL)
Any item that makes it possible, or easier, to carry out a task.

WEB SITES

For Web resources related to the subject of this book,
go to: www.windmillbooks.com/weblinks
and select this book's title.

READ MORE

Facklam, Margery. *What Does the Crow Know?: The Mysteries of Animal Intelligence*. Layton, UT: Gibbs Smith, Publisher, 2001.

Lunis, Natalie. *Crows*. Smart Animals. New York: Bearport Publishing, 2006.

Pringle, Laurence. *Crows! Strange and Wonderful*. Honesdale, PA: Boyds Mills Press, 2010.

INDEX